D1622346

THE INVISIBLE WOUNDS OF WAR

My Redemption

COL(RET.) BEVERLY SMITH-TILLERY

St. Petersburg Press

All attempts have been made to preserve the stories of the events, locales and conversations contained in this collection as the author remembers them. The author reserves the right to have changed the names of individuals and places if necessary and may have changed some identifying characteristics and details such as physical properties, occupations and places of residence in order to maintain their anonymity.

Published by St. Petersburg Press

St. Petersburg, FL

www.stpetersburgpress.com

Copyright ©2020

All rights reserved. No part of this publication may be reproduced, distributed, or transmitted in any form or by any means, including photocopying, recording or other electronic or mechanical methods, without the prior written permission of the publisher, except in the case of brief quotations embodied in critical reviews and certain other noncommercial uses permitted by copyright law. For permission requests contact St. Petersburg Press at www.stpetersburgpress.com.

Design and composition by St. Petersburg Press

Cover design by St. Petersburg Press and Pablo Guidi

Cover Photo *Shame [Image 5 of 5]*, U.S. Army Reserve Photo by Sgt. Audrey Hayes

Print ISBN: 978-1-940300-15-3

eBook ISBN: 978-1-940300-16-0

First Edition

THE INVISIBLE
WOUNDS OF WAR

"War may sometimes be a necessary evil. But no matter how necessary, it is always an evil, never a good. We will not learn how to live together in peace by killing each other's children."

Jimmy Carter

"Seeking to forget makes exile all the longer. The secret of redemption lies in remembrance."

Richard von Weizsacher

To the soldiers with whom I served.
To the soldiers who gave their lives to keep our country safe.
To the soldiers who came home but who fight the "Invisible Wounds of War".
To my sister Barbara who read every poem and made no judgements.
To my husband Mark who has been a pillar of support in my battle with
PTSD.

Acknowledgments

This project could not have been completed without the help of many people. I will do my best to not slight anyone. If by chance, I miss a fellow traveler in my long journey with PTSD and in compiling this book, please know that I am eternally grateful for all the help I received. First, I would like to thank my wonderful friend, Mr. Robert Driver. We have become confidants over the last two years. His encouragement kept me going on many long days. Our lively phone conversations broke up the monotony of hours of writing. My deepest appreciation is offered to my team of Beta Readers. They include: my sister Barbara Gray, who used her years of experience writing technical manuals to correct my punctuation, grammar and run on sentences; my special friend Tracy Solomon, who by her encouragement and praise made me feel that I could indeed finish this task; and my strong and steady friend Don Jensen, who made me know that God truly wanted this book finished. I would also like to thank my nephew Jamie Gray for the third and final title for my book. The path to completion of this book has been stressful and exhausting, but I have had a special person leading me along the way. That person is Amy J. Cianci, my Project Manager, at The St. Petersburg Press. Thank you, Amy, for believing in this work and for all your hours of patient listening. Lastly, I would like to thank my husband Mark Tillery, who went to war with me, understood the mental anguish of my PTSD and stood by me through the roughest times. During the writing of this book, he ate a lot of canned soup and brought me cups of coffee so I could keep going. He is the reason I get up every morning and walk the long road of living with PTSD.

Abbreviations

LRMC - Landstuhl Regional Medical Center is the largest US military hospital outside the continental United States. Located near Landstuhl, Germany, it serves as the nearest treatment center for wounded soldiers from Iraq and Afghanistan. Also serves as a stopover (medevacked via the nearby Ramstein Air Base) for serious casualties from Iraq and Afghanistan before being flown to the US. There is a myth at LRMC that the building was used by Hitler as the training site for his Youth Corps, as young as ten. The myth proposes that the US military obtained the building as a spoil of winning World War II. It is believed that the ghosts of those children walk the halls of LRMC.

PTSD - Post Traumatic Stress Disorder is a psychiatric disorder that can occur in people who have experienced or witnessed a traumatic event, such as a natural disaster, a serious accident, war/combat, rape or other violent personal assault. People with PTSD have intense, disturbing feelings related to their traumatic event that last long after the traumatic event has ended. They may relive the event through flashbacks or nightmares. They may feel sadness, fear, anger or guilt and feel detached or estranged from other people.

PONDS - Pond Security is a security service headquartered in Hesse, Germany. Founded by Daniel M. Pond in 1983 to guard railroads, airports and military installations.

D-Fac - Military slang for a Dining Facility.

Med-Cen - Military slang for a Medical Center.

MASH - The Mobile Army Surgical Hospital refers to a US Army medical unit serving as a fully functional hospital in a combat area of operations. The units were first established in 1945, and were deployed during the Korean War and other conflicts. The successor to MASH is the Combat Support Hospital (CSH).

BAMC - Brooke Army Medical Center is the US Army's premier medical institution. Located at Fort Sam Houston in San Antonio, Texas, it is a 425 bed Academic Medical Center and is the Department of Defense's largest facility. It is home to the US Army Institute of Surgical Research Burn Center.

VAMC - Veterans Affairs Medical Center

DDEAMC - Dwight David Eisenhower Army Medical Center is a 93 bed medical treatment facility located at Fort Gordon, Georgia near Augusta, Georgia. Active duty personnel and their beneficiaries use the medical center and clinics for their primary health care.

USERRA - The Uniform Services Employment and Reemployment Rights Act, passed in 1994, is a Federal statute that protects servicemembers' and veterans' civilian employment rights. It specifically safeguards the civilian employment of reserve military personnel in the US called to active duty. More information about USERRA can be found at https://www.justice.gov/crt-military/userra-statute.

ESGR - The Employer Support of the Guard and Reserve is the lead US Defense Department program promoting cooperation and understanding between civilian employers and their National Guard and Reserve employees. ESGR's primary means for mediating workplace conflict is its Ombudsman Services Program.

1st Loo-ey - Army slang for First Lieutenant military rank.

LTC - Lieutenant Colonel military rank.

Photo note

With two exceptions, all photographs in this book are the personal photos of the author or have been reprinted with the permission of the Department of Defense. The DoD photos are taken of active duty service personnel by active duty service personnel. We thank all branches of the U.S. Military represented by those photographers and photo subjects for contributing to this journey.

Introduction

I know that many readers skip a book's Introduction. I have done this many times only to realize that valuable insights may be gained from reading those one or two pages. I wrote this Introduction after completing my book to summarize its contents and pique your interest. I hope that you will take the time to read it.

I never thought that I would write poetry, write a book about my wartime experiences or be writing this Introduction. It always amazes me how life changes.

The event that has most impacted my life was my six years of wartime service. Soldiers don't just go to war, come home and carry on. War is a life-changing experience. The physical injuries I sustained in the war have presented challenges. The emotional injuries I sustained in the war were much more challenging. My diagnosis of Post-Traumatic Stress Disorder is a life-long, life-altering disorder that can be moderated, but not cured.

In the Civil War, PTSD was called "Soldier's Heart", in World War I "Shell Shock", in World War II and the Korean War "Battle Fatigue" or "Combat Exhaustion". In 1980, the diagnosis known as PTSD was developed. Vietnam War veterans were the first to have the term PTSD applied to them. Veterans of Operation Iraqi Freedom/Operation Enduring Freedom (shortened to the Iraq/Afghanistan Wars in this book) suffer at a rate of 12-30%. This is more than 300,000 soldiers.

After extensive treatment for my PTSD over the course of four years, I turned to poetry writing to deal with my wartime memories. Compiling my poems and writing the history of my wartime experiences have been additional steps.

This book contains two articles by Mr. Robert Driver. My collection of poems follows. A short introduction precedes each poem to put them into the context of my military career. The next section details my trip to the National Veterans Creative Arts Festival as a national gold medal winner in poetry writing. Following that is factual information about PTSD and veteran suicide with resources for treatment. All the profit I may realize from the sale of this book will be donated to worthy causes. This is explained at the end of the book.

If you are making the journey with PTSD, as I am, I want you to know that there is hope and help and peace. This book documents my journey. Godspeed on your journey.

Articles by Robert Driver

At our home in Florida, I eagerly await the arrival of our local newspaper *The Seminole Beacon*. It is tossed on our lawn, out of a slow-moving car, every Thursday morning. I immediately open it to a column entitled "Driver's Seat" by Bob Driver. Bob's writing is candid, thought-provoking, and touched with a dry sense of humor. I contacted Bob in 2018 to compliment him on his columns. We became fast friends. Then I sought his advice on writing this book. He was highly encouraging and said, "Go for it and don't be afraid." Two of his articles, "To Write, do you have to be scared?" and "Some thoughts on poets and poetry" were instrumental in my decision to write this book. His second article is particularly poignant. In it he arrives at a private conclusion about poetry that he doesn't understand. He concludes that the poet was writing only for himself. For two years, I wrote poetry only for myself. It was an outlet to put to rest my many disturbing memories of war and to deal with my PTSD. It was Bob Driver who led me to believe that it was time to share my poems. I have included the articles and hope you enjoy reading them.

To write, do we have to be scared?

Driver's Seat
Bob Driver

At last count, 4,911 books have been published about how to write, what to write, how to write better, how to sell what you write and even how to think about writing.

One of the most informative of these instruction manuals is "The Courage to Write," by author Ralph Keyes, researched, read and interviewed dozens of writers. In the process he learned much about the connections between courage, fear and writing.

These connections are real, not imaginary. Keyes' findings and opinions are alarming, and in some ways discouraging. By the time I finished reading "The Courage to Write" I found myself wondering "How in the world does any writer have the guts to even begin?"

I don't have the skill, wisdom, experience and wide-ranging knowledge that Keyes possesses. Even so, I believe that in at least one sentence of his book Keyes overstated his case. On page 13, Keyes flat-out says "If you're not scared, you're not writing."

I don't think that's true. I concede that gathering facts and ideas, and then assembling them into clear sentences, can be filled with uncertainty and tension. But there is no absolute principle that says to all writers, "You'd better be scared, buster. If you're not, then you're not really writing."

In my far-from-glorious years as a writer, I've worked beside dozens of colleagues who gave little or no evidence that fear must be an inevitable companion of the act of writing. I saw those writers coping with dozens of problems

and snarls that can enter into producing worthwhile examples of the English language. But as I watched them I saw little evidence of these writers being "scared" of the act of writing.

This absence of "writing" fear was most prevalent in the newspapers I worked for. By the time most journalists get ready to write they will have gathered and sorted out the facts they intend to present to the public. The words are there, in the writer's notes and brain. The blank typewriter page or computer screen is ready. The world is waiting. It's show time, folks.

In news work, the fear of the actual writing process is usually crowded out by a much larger fear: the deadline. This tool was invented by a caveman king in 14,368 B.C. His name was Uggh, and he wanted his latest proclamation to be chiseled in stone by noon next Thursday. He told his chiselers, "Do it, or die!" They did it, and the deadline has been an inspirational device used ever since.

Equally fearsome in newswriting are loathsome editors, especially city editors named Joe or John. I spent three years in a northern newsroom feeding Joe. He was a two-Prussian

who loved to excoriate and humble his reporters for little reasons or none at all. He won the ultimate middle-finger salute: his staff hated him so much we made sure we never took our vacation at the same time Joe did. We wanted every possible hour of distance between us.

John was a sneaky little arschloch (a German word whose English meaning is easily found via Google. He controlled his newsroom by simply firing anyone who crossed him. One day he chose the wrong victim, who exposed John's Nazi tactics to our previously unaware publisher. Two days later John was gone. Our newsroom exploded in more joy than I had witnessed since V-J Day.

Please forgive these two memory-lane accounts, above. They're the only bad-editor anecdotes I have in my literary memory. Most editors are also writers, and want to help their troops, not hinder them.

Also, upon reviewing my remarks about John Keyes and "The Courage to Write," I should have pointed out that most of his comments apply to fiction writers and poets, rather than to non-fiction writers. Fiction is an open door to a dozen forms of fear, and Keyes masterfully describes them all. Whether you're planning to write a short story or a 400-page novel, I suggest that you acquaint yourself with Keyes' wisdom. He will tell you what you're in for, as well as how to survive it.

Bob Driver's email address is tralee71@comcast.net.

Originally Published In *Tampa Bay Newspaper's Weekly Seminole Beacon* on April 25, 2019

Some thoughts on poets and poetry

Driver's Seat
Bob Driver

Don't panic. As you read the title of this piece you may be tempted to hurry onward to the next item, to avoid getting entangled in a super-clearly dissertation on what poetry is and is not. Relax. I have neither the brains nor the discipline to be a poet or an authority on poetry.

In fact, I'm not sure if I've ever met more than three or four honest-to-God poets in my lifetime. They're the ones who work for years at practicing their craft by not only writing poems but actually submitting them for publication and pay. Sad to say, of all forms of writing, poetry may be the least likely to be financial rewarding.

Or, in many cases, least likely to understand. The first "poem" most of us encounter is a nursery rhyme. Jack and Jill went up the hill. Little Miss Muffet sat on a tuffet... and so on. By high school we may have graduated to Poe and "The Raven." Most of this mid-level poetry met two requirements: (1) It contained an actual rhyme scheme, and (2) it was understandable.

But then we run into the big boys and girls: Keats, Byron, Shelley, Mr. and Mrs. Browning and so on. As the quality of the writing climbed, so did the readers' need for patience, persistence and clear thinking if we were to grasp the meaning of the poet's words. And that's where so many of us stopped reading poetry.

Or at least some modern versions, such as the rarified poems published in the New Yorker

and other outlets. Occasionally I'll tackle one of them. I congratulate myself when I fathom even a few of the allusions and references contained in the poem.

When I suspect that the poet is playing a meaningless joke on the reader, I arrive at a private conclusion: the poet was writing for himself alone, without any concern for the reader's understanding.

I felt that way a couple of nights ago when I viewed a DVD honoring the words and music of the Canadian-born Leonard Cohen. While lacking the rawness of many entertainers, Cohen was able to forge a distinctive style that gradually turned him into a cult figure by the time of his death two years ago at age 82.

As I listened to his songs, I wrote down snatches of his lyrics for further contemplation. I may be mistaken, but some of his words seem destined to have no link between his own mind and the outside world. And that's okay, I suppose. After all, the gap was a poet, so what the hell.

This seemed true even for a Cohen

masterpiece: "Hallelujah." I first heard that song a few nights after the 2016 presidential election. It was rendered by the lovely Saturday Night Live comic genius Kate McKinnon. The song stirred me, but I'm still not sure why. I've heard that Cohen wrote and re-wrote "Hallelujah" over the course of years. If you want to learn what the lyrics mean for may have meant) you'd better lean on Google. I'm not enough of a mystic to offer my own translation, even if I had one in mind.

To launch your own foray into the lush wilderness of serious poetry, pick up a copy of the Gwyneth Paltrow film "Possession," it's based on a novel by the same name, written by A.S. Byatt, an acclaimed British novelist. It won the 1990 Booker prize, the most prestigious literary award available in the English-speaking world.

The mystery-romance plot describes how a pair of young literary scholars uncovered and disclosed a scandalous love affair between two Victorian poets. Heart-pounding stuff? Not at all. Just mighty fine writing.

Or you can try one of my favorite books, "Good Poems," collected by Garrison Keillor, the sage of Lake Wobegon. The contents are a mix of old and modern poetry, all of it comprehensible to us groundlings. Enjoy.

Bob Driver's email address is tralee71@comcast.net.

Originally Published In *Tampa Bay Newspaper's Weekly Seminole Beacon* on October 17, 2018

Journey to War

WHEN I WAS COMMISSIONED in the US Army Nurse Corps as a First Lieutenant in 1988, I was thirty-nine years old. I was eligible to join because the age limit for the Nurse Corps had recently been extended from thirty-seven to forty-two years. I always felt like an "old soldier". The majority of soldiers with whom I served were so much younger than me. Before the invasion of Iraq on March 20, 2003, I had served as a Reserve soldier. I always thought that I would probably never go to war.

Prior to the second invasion of Iraq, the Army made the decision to upgrade the skills of the Army Combat Medic, labeled 91B, from EMT to Paramedic level. After lengthy courses and skills training, these soldiers would be known as Health Care Specialist, labeled 68W. The Army knew that the casualties coming off the battlefields of Iraq and Afghanistan would have complicated and devastating injuries. The belief was that with the advanced skills provided by the 68W, the chances of survival for those soldiers would be greatly improved. The courses the 91B took for this transition were heavily weighted in combat casualty care, because of the impending re-invasion of Iraq and the seemingly unending war in

Afghanistan. At the completion of their training, the 68W was required to take and pass the civilian National EMT exam.

In early 2000, I was tasked to open a school to uptrain Army Reserve and National Guard 91Bs to 68W. I taught there from 2000-2003, fully knowing that my students would be taking their skills to the battlefield. When I looked at my 91B students, I saw young faces, ages 19 to early 30's. At 54 years old, I again felt like an old soldier. However, we were all going to war. The poem that follows is a preamble to my deployment to war.

U.S. Air Force Photo by Tech. Sgt. Erik Gudmundson

Poem - Journey to War

Is it harder if you go to war
When you are young or when you're old?
Is it better to face sights of war
With aging eyes or innocence?
Before the war I trained my troops
In better skills for battlefields.
As medics they'd be on the ground
When shots rang out, soldiers went down.
I told them if war's not for you
To just get out, before the fight.
And one young man with worried frown
Stopped me one day and stammered out,
"Ma'am, I don't think this is for me."
I nodded and I wished him well.
Then all of us went off to war,
To Iraq and Afghanistan.
And six years later I came home
When I retired at sixty-one.
It seemed I'd been the oldest one,
A soldier serving with the young.

Years later I flew out of town,
At TSA at the airport,
A young man just said, "Mornin', Ma'am."
It had a distinct Army ring.
I looked at him in puzzlement.
His long Dredd locks plus fifty pounds
Disguised the young man I had known.
I said to him, "Do I know you?"
He said, "I was your soldier, Ma'am."
His buddy laughed and said, "No way,
You never were a soldier, man!"
The young man snapped to attention
And gave me a perfect salute.
I rendered him back my salute.
His buddy said, "Well, I'll be damned.
I guess you were a soldier, man."
The young man said, "Ma'am, I regret
The choice I made that fated day."
I said, "War's not for everyone."
He nodded and I wished him well.
Is it harder if you go to war
When you are young or when you're old?
Is it better to face sights of war
With aging eyes or innocence?
Or harder to live with the guilt
Because you chose to stay at home?

No Battle Line

I WAS STATIONED at Landstuhl Regional Medical Center in Germany from 2006-2009. This is the large trauma center that receives the wounded and ill soldiers from the battlefields of Iraq and Afghanistan. Care was provided there, not only for US soldiers, but also for the coalition soldiers, such as the British, Romanians and Australians; for civilian contractors, such as employees of Blackwater Security; and for news media, such as a National Geographic team and a FOX News reporter. We provided maternity care for soldiers and military dependents from all over Europe. In addition, it serves military personnel stationed throughout Europe and Africa, as well as their family members.

My family was grateful that, for those two years, I was not deployed to a combat zone. However, LRMC was not a safe place. It was considered the "softest" terrorist target in Europe. There were hidden dangers that lurked on the grounds and in the four miles of hallways. During my time at Landstuhl, many incidents made this very clear to me. The poem that follows demonstrates that there is no front line or safe zone during war time.

The author at the entrance to military housing at LRMC
2006

U.S. Army photo showing the vast complex of buildings
that make up the miles-long LRMC treatment facility.

Landstuhl Regional Medical Center (LRMC)

Hospital System: United States Army Medical Command
Located: Landstuhl, Rhineland-Palatinate, Germany
Founded: 1953
Size: 310 beds
Motto: "Selfless Service"
Current Commander: Colonel Timothy L. Hudson

Poem - No Battle Line

We liked to think that we were safe,
We always knew that we were not.
Atop a hill in Germany,
A chain link fence to keep war out
And German PONDS guards, mostly old.
We knew we were a soft target,
In all of Europe number one.
We'd work and try to be as safe
As we could be with constant threats.
The day that soldiers from Airborne
Surrounded Landstuhl with Humvees
To protect those who had survived
A bloody battle in Iraq.
After they'd killed the eight downrange,
Al-qaeda promised to make sure
Those left alive they would take out.
The Sergeant from the Airborne team
Told me his men would stop that threat.
They kept their guard for four long days
Until their soldiers made it home.

My friend, a PONDS guard, named Irene
Would often stop me as I left
The Med-Cen in the dark for home.
She'd say, "This night is dangerous.
Stay in your room and don't go out."
She never told me what was wrong,
But I would heed the words she gave.
When terrorists had hatched a plan
To blow up eight planes U.S. bound,
In London stopped at their plan's end.
The police searched their apartments
And found the floor plans for Landstuhl.
I knew that they had stolen them
Because of what Irene had said,
That two men caught inside Landstuhl,
Were taking pictures of floor plans,
One man was caught, the other fled.
One day I slept from night on call,
Arose at noon to get some food,
In blue jeans and an old sweatshirt,
My ID in my front pocket,
I left my room for the D-Fac.
I saw a soldier in the hall,
Accompanied by bomb-sniffing dog,
The soldier wore his Kevlar vest,
His helmet and his M-16.
He wheeled as I came out the door,
The M-16 right at my chest.
I spread my arms as I'd been trained,
I froze and said in shaking voice,
"Good morning, soldier, my ID
Is right here in my left pocket."
In shaking voice, he said to me,
"Ma'am, take it out with two fingers."
After he looked at my ID,
He said, "Thanks, ma'am. Please carry on."

My heart was pounding in my chest
And I knew I'd been close to death.
I never knew why he had come,
What threat was lurking in the halls.
I still don't like the dark of night
Where terror lurks and danger strikes.
I guess you take the fears along
Home with you even after war.

A Day in the Anesthesia
Department at LRMC

IN THE ANESTHESIA department at LRMC, I served as a nurse anesthetist (66F) in the OR. The anesthesia personnel on duty had a short staff meeting each morning before we started our cases. Announcements were made and cases for the day were reviewed. We sat in the anesthesia staff lounge, sleepily sipping our coffee, before the start of another long stressful day.

A medical person in the military has two distinct roles. The first is to provide care which is your specialty. In that role, you belong to a department. There is a chain of command for the department. In my case, that was the Anesthesia Department, which was headed by the Chief of Anesthesia. The second role is that of soldier. In my role of soldier at LRMC, I belonged to Charlie Company. Some of my soldier activities were preparing for and passing a physical fitness test, maintaining weapons qualifications and submitting to drug testing. My chain of command was headed by a Company Commander, who often did not have a medical background, but who was well grounded in soldier management. At times this was an extremely conflicting dilemma. If a soldier activity, such as being drug tested, occurred at 4:00 AM, then the day working in the Anesthesia Department ended at 1:00 AM the next morning, it resulted in a 21 hour work day. My First Sergeant for Charlie Company was 1SGT Corey Barnes. He was an outstanding First Sergeant, who was efficient and organized, but also personable and approachable. 1SGT Barnes was one of the best soldiers with whom I ever served. He had just recently returned to LRMC from a deployment to Iraq, where he had served as a decorated Combat Medic.

One morning, not long after my deployment to LRMC, the atmosphere in the anesthesia lounge before morning staff meeting was very different. There was a palpable tension in the air. The anesthesiologist, who was in charge of "running the board"(scheduling cases, setting priority for case order, etc.) came in for our meeting with a grim and haggard look on his face. We knew that he had news that would impact us all. The news was heartbreaking.

I was the last person in the Anesthesia Department to speak with 1SGT Barnes. I felt so much guilt, thinking that I had missed a hint about his decision. Had I missed an opportunity to intervene? A big component of PTSD is the burden of guilt we carry.

The following poem is written in memory of 1SGT Corey Barnes.[1]

Sgt Corey R. Barnes

Birth 28 Dec 1978
Lancaster, Los Angeles County, California, USA
Death 14 Jun 2006 (aged 27)
Germany
Burial Our Mother of Sorrows Cemetery
Reno, Washoe County, Nevada, USA
Plot Garden of Resurrection, BB 5
Memorial ID 14660548

---

1. *Find A Grave*, database and images (https://www.findagrave.com : accessed 02
December 2019), memorial page for Sgt Corey R. Barnes (28 Dec 1978–14 Jun
2006), Find A Grave Memorial no. 14660548, citing Our Mother of Sorrows
Cemetery, Reno, Washoe County, Nevada, USA ; Maintained by dot (contributor
46604592).

Poem - A Day in the Anesthesia Department at LRMC

In Memoriam: 1SGT Corey Barnes, passed away June 14, 2006, age 27
Morning report
Before we start
A day of work,
We sip our coffee and exchange a word or two.

Today is odd
The air is tense
Our chief is grim,
We wait for news that we don't really want to hear.

Chief clears his throat
Says "Listen up,
I have bad news,
Our sergeant hung himself last night in his bedroom."

A gasp of shock
A cry of pain
A question "Why?"

We know a trip downrange can do that to a man.

I'm filled with guilt
I saw him last
He spoke to me,
What if I missed a clue that could have saved his life?

Two days have passed
We sit in rows
To show respect,
To honor a good soldier taken tragically.

His name is called
No answer back
His name is called,
In silence I can hear the sobs, can feel the pain.

Morning report
We all go on
Holes in our hearts,
I won't forget the last day that he called me "Ma'am."

Dreams of LRMC

SOME OF THE longest hours of my life were spent on night call for the Anesthesia Department at LRMC. I carried four pagers: one for calls to a cardiac arrest; one for calls to the Emergency Department; one for calls to maternity to put in an epidural for a laboring mother or to provide anesthesia for a c-section; and one for calls to provide pain management. I also provided anesthesia care in the OR if a case was in progress. Needless to say, this was often quite a juggling act. I had a bed in the Recovery Room, where I would doze, when I wasn't called to provide care. I rarely had an opportunity to need that bed. There were four miles of hallways and three stories at LRMC. A big part of my night was spent walking the long miles from one area of the hospital to the other and running up and down stairwells.

Near one of the trauma wards, called 8C/D, were snack machines. I was always over there at night checking the machines for honey buns and Snickers candy bars. I always had a pocket full of coins at the ready. The window sills at LRMC were low to the floor and wide enough to sit on. Since the building was so over-heated in the winter, I would often sit on a window sill at night and press my face against the cold pane of glass. The irony was that, even though it seemed that heat was never rationed, electricity must have been. All unneeded lighting was turned off at night. In the dim and shadowy hallways, I often thought I saw the ghosts of Hitler's boy soldiers.

I have a recurring dream of my nights on call at LRMC. Most of the dreams I have in connection with the war are painful and disturbing. However, after this dream, I wake up feeling calm and at peace.

The following poem will let you share a night of call with me.

Poem - Dreams of LRMC

I walk the halls
Of Landstuhl in my dreams.
In green scrub suit
With pagers at my side.

The shadows loom
Like ghosts of Hitler's youth,
Who came to learn
The lies of Nazi truth.

But now this place
Takes soldiers who come in
With wounds from wars
In mountains and in sand.

I press my face
On windowpane ice cold.
There are no stars
To brighten German nights.

My aching legs
Remind me that I'm tired.
I sit and rest,
I think of going home.

I see a chair,
It's rolling down the hall.
He comes to me
And says,"Ma'am, you're out late."

I smile at him,
Say, "Soldier, you are too."
And then I see
He's missing both his legs.

I put my hand
On his hand, then I say,
"I'm so sorry."
Then he says, "It's okay,
The price of war,
Don't need them anyway."

We sit in peace,
This soldier boy and me.
The night is dim,
We think of going home.

Each night I hope
That sleep will come to me,
I walk the halls
Of Landstuhl in my dreams.

The Gaelic Soldier

SOMETIMES IT SEEMS that the faces of the hundreds of soldiers I cared for at LRMC are just a blur. However, there are times when I recall a very specific face and memory. Throughout this book, I will introduce you to some of those soldiers. This does not mean that they were more important than those other soldiers who required my anesthesia services. I gave each and every one of them my fullest attention and compassionate care. However, I have a difficult time putting some memories to rest. Those soldiers are the subject of repeat dreams and flashbacks, all a part of the PTSD syndrome. I found that writing a poem about a disturbing memory would give me peace and allow me to stop its recurring dream.

In the following poem, I would like you to meet a young Canadian soldier of Gaelic descent, who fought alongside the American soldiers in Iraq.

Poem - The Gaelic Soldier

His close-cropped hair was coal black,
And his eyes were violet,
So handsome and so striking,
That I looked away in shame.

He said, "Mornin', ma'am" to me,
In a soft distinctive brogue,
Then said, "Ma'am, I am Gaelic
And I hail from Canada."

I said, "Do you speak Gaelic?"
He said, "I learned as a lad,
Sitting on my Grammy's lap,
From lullabies she sang."

"So say some words in Gaelic,
Then we're off to the O.R."
"I'll say the words my Gram would say,
Right before she left the bar."

In Gaelic, smiling, he said,
"Please pour me another pint."
Both of us had quite a laugh,
I pushed him down the hall.

I never saw him again,
But I think of him at times,
I know it broke Grammy's heart,
When he finally came home.

Her laddie came back from war,
He was handsome and so brave,
But he'd never be the same,
He was missing both his legs.

War in the Desert

THE ORIGIN of the quotation "There are no atheists in foxholes" is uncertain. The US military chaplain William Thomas Cummings may have said it in a field sermon during the Battle of Bataan in 1942. Other sources credit it to statements made at the end of World War I. I personally believe in a Divine Being, as do most of our American military. Less than one percent of military members select "Atheist" as their religious preference. During the war, I often wondered where God was. The horrors of war made me feel that God had deserted me. What God could allow the things to happen that I witnessed?

In war there is often a feeling of isolation. Even surrounded by my fellow soldiers, I often felt alone. Part of that feeling is related to being separated from family and friends from civilian life. Part of that feeling may be related to a lack of support from those very same people. I encountered this in talking to my injured soldiers. Some had no one back home to notify of their arrival at LRMC.

The poem that follows is a cry of desperation to God or a Supreme Being for deliverance from the horrors of war. It also poignantly expresses the feelings of isolation felt by many soldiers.

Poem - War in the Desert

I gaze out at the shimmering sand,
At smoke from oil wells burning there,
I cry "Hosanna, do you hear?"
But only silence answers me.

Hijab clad women stop and stare,
Then flee to safety from the bombs,
I shout, "Mohammed, are you near?"
But empty streets are all I see.

We're left alone here to survive,
A band of soldiers holding on,
On one another to depend,
To fight a war we cannot win.

Christ, God, Jehovah,
Take me home.

Department of Defense photo by Lance Cpl. James F.
Cline III, USMC

IED Blast in Iraq

IF I THINK about all the soldiers I provided anesthesia care for during the war, the young man in the following poem was probably my most devastating. He and his five buddies left their base camp one morning in Iraq on patrol. Their Humvee hit an IED on the roadway. The blast and ensuing fire killed his five buddies at the scene. The fire burned the surviving soldier horribly. When he arrived at LRMC, I was shocked that he was still alive. His arms and legs had already been amputated by the MASH team in Iraq. In the OR, we cleaned and dressed his burns.

As soon as it was known that a burn victim was arriving, The Burn Team from BAMC in San Antonio, Texas was notified. They immediately left BAMC on a flight to Germany to transfer our soldier to the Army's premier burn center. The team from BAMC arrived while I still had the young soldier in the operating room. When he was in my care, I looked at his Army ID card and the picture of his face was planted in my brain. When he was stable after surgery, he was put on a flight to Texas.

The Army *Stars and Stripes* newspaper had a lengthy front page article about those six young soldiers. There were many pictures of them in their housing in Iraq. They showed them horsing around.

One of them was strumming a guitar. The article gave information about their time together and the tragedy that had claimed the lives of five of them. I watched the *Stars and Stripes* everyday for updates on the one surviving member of the group. Twelve days after his injury, he died at BAMC. I often wondered why he survived so long. I ached over the agony his family must have felt at the extent of damage an IED can cause. Did they need to resolve some prior issue before they could let him go? Did they just need time to say good-by?

My memory of him is one of my hardest to put to rest. Even now, I don't believe I have made peace with it. The following poem recounts the decision I made that day and the journey of that young soldier.

Department of Defense Photo by Lance Cpl. Alison
Dostie, USMC

Poem - I.E.D. Blast in Iraq

One hot dry morning in Iraq
They left on their patrol,
The I.E.D. killed five buddies
And he alone survived.

The MASH team took his arms and legs
And sent me what was left,
In the O.R. in Germany
We worked to clean his burns.

The face he'd had was burned away,
I looked at his I.D.
I saw the face of just a boy,
Too young to go to war.

I thought, "I could just let him go,"
Then thought, "You are not God."
The Burn Team came from San Antone
To take the soldier home.

He lived for twelve days in the States,
I often wondered why.
And then he joined his five buddies,
Where all brave soldiers go.

They buried him at Arlington,
Full honors for his life.
I often dream of that young man
And often see his face.

I wake with pillow drenched in tears,
An aching in my heart,
P.T.S.D.'s the price I pay,
It leaves long lasting scars.

My Husband, My Hero

FOR TWO OF the six years I served on active duty for the war, my husband Mark Tillery was able to accompany me. When he arrived at LRMC, after I had settled in, we looked at volunteer activities for him to fill his days. I talked to the Chaplaincy Service about Mark serving in the Wounded Warrior Ministry as an unpaid civilian volunteer. Chaplain Harp immediately said, "Can he start to work tomorrow?" So Mark served in the Wounded Warrior Ministry, more commonly called the Clothes Closet, for two years. He also volunteered as a Ward Secretary on one of the trauma wards because the full-time civilian employee was having a complicated pregnancy.

During those years, he worked up to eighteen hours a day and thirty-two days in a row. I was keeping the same hours and days in the Operating Room. LRMC was the receiving hospital for the casualties off the battlefields of Iraq and Afghanistan. Up to three planes a day, carrying up to sixty soldiers each, could arrive at Ramstein Air Force Base nearby. The Chaplaincy Service had five buildings stocked with warm clothing, shoes, pajamas, toiletries and calling cards donated by the American public. Many of our soldiers came in wearing a patient gown or part of their uniform and barefoot. Mark could outfit a soldier from head to toe including under-wear, socks and a warm jacket or hoodie. There were quilts of valor made by American women and blankets made by American chil-dren. We called those blankets "snugglies" because the soldiers would come to the OR snuggled in them. They would ask to be put to sleep holding them. This request was always granted. Many items were donated by American professional sports teams with their logos. These items were particularly coveted by the soldiers. The coalition countries, such as England, Poland and Canada, gave substantial cash donations.

Mark offered the soldiers the opportunity to talk about what preyed on their minds, such as the loss of buddies downrange or receiving "Dear John" letters from wives or girlfriends. Some soldiers would come to the Clothes Closet everyday just to talk to Mark. In order to make them feel needed, he would give them small jobs to do. If they expressed a need, he would pray with them. Mark had Bibles, Torah and Korans to pass out. He was quite flexible in praying in any denomination. In the afternoons, when the incoming injured and sick soldiers had tapered off, he would take a cart stocked with items to the trauma, medical and psychiatric wards for the soldiers unable to make the trip to him.

Mark gave tours of the Wounded Warrior Ministry to: digni-taries, such as generals and admirals from the Pentagon and ambas-sadors; political figures, such as Hillary Clinton and Nancy Pelosi; and celebrities, such as Gary Sinese and the Band of Brothers. He toured company commanders to inform them about Clothes Closet supplies available for their soldiers. Mark wanted everyone to see what the American people were doing for the soldiers and how much it was appreciated.

Mark received many "Commanders' Coins", which are beauti-fully decorated coins presented by senior military leadership to show their appreciation for a phenomenal job. It is more than just a thank you or pat on the back. It is something tangible to remember the moment by. He also received many awards for his volunteer activi-ties at LRMC. These included: U.S. Army Garrison Kaiserslautern Volunteer of the Quarter in 2006, U.S. Army Garrison Kaiserslautern Volunteer of the Year in 2007, President's Volunteer Service Award, Certificate of Appreciation from Secretary of the Interior Dirk Kempthorne, Certificate of Appreciation from the Chief of Pastoral Services, Certificate of Appreciation from the American Red Cross and Certificate of Recognition from the Veterans of Foreign Wars.

Mark became the go-to-person for soldiers' needs at LRMC. There was no one at LRMC who did not know and appreciate Mark. He would like to thank Chaplains Griffin and Harp for giving him the opportunity to serve the thousand soldiers per month who came through the Wounded Warrior Ministry.

The following poem is written in honor of my husband, Mark Tillery, my hero.

To William Tillery with Best Wishes!

December 2007

With the Compliments of
The Secretary of the Interior

DIRK KEMPTHORNE

Mark Tillery being honored by Secretary for the Interior,
Dirk Kempthorne in 2007 and U.S. Army Garrison
Kaiserslautern in 2006 for his service as a Civilian
Volunteer

Mark Tillery serving in the Wounded Warrior Ministry
Clothes Closet 2007

Poem - My Husband, My Hero

My husband, Mark, is my hero,
He wasn't called, but went to war,
In Germany for two long years,
He volunteered with Chaplaincy.
In a place known as Clothes Closet,
He served the soldiers from downrange.
As soldiers came in off the planes,
The "Walking Wounded" from the wars,
He made sure they had what they need,
From clothing, phone cards, valor quilts.
The heat in Iraq was intense,
But Germany was freezing cold,
The soldiers came in just a gown,
Often with no shoes on their feet.
Mark often worked eighteen hours straight,
Not leaving until all were served.
He offered them a place to talk,
Of terrors seen and buddies lost,
He'd offer Bibles, Torah too,
And also Koran to a few.

And if they felt a need to pray,
He stood with them and held their hands.
Some came each day to visit him,
A place of safety in wars' storms,
He'd give them little jobs to do,
So they'd feel useful and return.
Mark would come home on a long day,
And wonder when the war would end.
On one cold rainy German night,
We heard a knock on our front door,
A soldier seeking help from Mark,
To outfit soldiers who'd come in.
The two soldiers were honor guard
For dead soldiers brought from Iraq.
They'd stopped at LRMC overnight,
Then on to Dover the next day.
Mark said, "No problem, I'll be there,"
Left in the rain to outfit them.
With warm clothes, toiletries and snacks,
The two soldiers were good to go.
When Mark returned I said to him,
"You are my hero" and he laughed,
He said, "No, I just do my job."
Then after two years, we came home,
Left his volunteer job behind,
But never did he forget those,
Who came from war to Clothes Closet.

The Guilt of War

THIS YOUNG SOLDIER'S story is one that broke my heart. He told me of an incident in Iraq that left me shocked and shattered. It was a cold, rainy and dreary day when he arrived at LRMC. It had been a quiet afternoon when he arrived in the operating room. The wounds to his lower legs were minor in comparison to the many devastating injuries we often received. I remember thinking, "Just an easy anesthesia case and then I can go home." When I reached out to touch the soldier's hand, I realized that this situation was much more complicated.

The soldiers downrange often consume large quantities of sports drinks that are high in caffeine and are very dehydrating. This can result in serious and even fatal complications when combined with anesthesia. The soldiers use these drinks to stay alert on patrol or stay awake for long hours on sentry duty. I thought that this was the situation with this young soldier and proceeded to take measures to make his impending anesthesia safer. The surgeon, who was waiting to do the surgery, was very impatient to get the case done so he could go home. I had to keep him at bay while I worked with the young man. Then, the soldier told me his devastating secret which was the deeper cause of his anxiety and distress.

I know that guilt is often a major underlying component of PTSD. Soldiers ask themselves questions like, "Why did I come home and my buddies didn't? Could I have done more to keep them safe? Why did I deserve to live and another soldier did not survive? Where was God on that fateful day? When will I be able to go back and join my unit?" I have asked myself many of these same questions. It is only by working through these feelings of guilt that we can lay to rest the "invisible wounds of war".

The following poem shows the guilt that can follow us home from the battlefield.

Department of Defense Photo by Navy Petty Officer 1st Class Spencer Fling

Poem - The Guilt of War

He came in from the battlefield,
A cold and wet November day,
His leg wounds were not serious,
And so I thought, an easy case,
We'll make a quick trip to OR
And then a quick recovery.
I reached to touch his shaking hand,
But he flinched and then pulled away.
I told him that I'd meant no harm,
He said, "Ma'am, I would like your touch
But I am dirty and I stink,
I've had no bath in many weeks."
I told him that I didn't care,
And then I reached to touch his wrist,
And there I was surprised to find,
His heart rate was 200 plus,
His lips were dry and they were cracked
And so I gave him IV fluids,
I asked him how many sports drinks
That he would drink in just a day,

He said, "I've been on guard duty,
And if I sleep, I'll wake up dead."
He said that he drank six Red Bulls
And four Kick Starts and Monster Juice.
The caffeine helped him stay awake.
I now knew why his rate was fast,
I started with the drug Versed.
He dozed, then startled back awake,
I told him, "Soldier, now you're safe."
And then he said in trembling voice,
"I need to tell you something, Ma'am.
Along side an Iraqi guard,
I was on night watch in a tower,
He lit a cigarette to smoke,
I told him he must put it out,
We're sitting ducks, but he refused,
And so I killed him with my knife."
I was so shocked at what he'd said,
But made sure I showed no alarm,
I told him, "Soldier, God forgives
The things we do to survive war."
I took him to the OR suite
And then I put him off to sleep,
The only sleep he'd had in days.
The guilt of war all soldiers share
Will haunt us 'til our dying day.

Post-Traumatic Stress Disorder

EVEN BEFORE I came home from the war, I was having symptoms of Post-Traumatic Stress Disorder. I witnessed very upsetting incidents during my first active duty call-up to Fort Gordon in Augusta, Georgia. I was mobilized there to provide anesthesia care for the many soldiers injured in the training activities preceding the second invasion of Iraq. It was necessary to get these surgeries done before the influx of injured soldiers expected stateside from Iraq. Some of these training injuries were devastating and career-ending. My second mobilization was to Fort Campbell, Kentucky, to provide anesthesia for soldiers from the 101st Airborne. They needed surgical procedures done before their return to Iraq for another deployment. Most of these soldiers had already been to war, some multiple times. While they were incredibly brave when facing the dangers of war, they were terrified when facing surgery and anesthesia. They would open up and talk to me about loss of their buddies, the guilt of leaving their wives and small children again, and fear of not coming home. There was very little relief I could give them, except to listen.

Then I volunteered for four years of active duty. The two and a half years I was stationed at LRMC saw the onset of my PTSD symptoms. I had seen horrifying injuries off the battlefields of Iraq and Afghanistan. I had experienced grief at not being able to save every soldier. I had felt anger at the life changing injuries I had seen. I had worked bone exhausting series of hours and days in the OR and on emergency night call, that would never be tolerated in a civilian setting. While pushing a 380 pound civilian contractor, who had encountered a suicide bomber in Iraq to the OR, I ruptured a disc in my neck. This required a surgical repair. Within two weeks of my first surgery, I had an emergency surgery for a kidney stone. The surgery was unsuccessful, and the ensuing complications nearly cost me my life. On a visit to the Urology Clinic, I was sexually assaulted by my surgeon. I did not report the incident because my promotion was being considered by the Promotion Board. I did not want to jeopardize my chances of promotion to Colonel.

After my surgeries, I had long hours alone in my housing to think about what I had seen in the war. I was ridden with guilt because I was not able to take care of the incoming wounded. I had bottles of Oxycodone prescribed for post-operative pain and a ready supply of German wine. I used them to ease my guilt over not being able to work and bury my anxiety over my complicated recovery. I was now set up for PTSD. I finally sought help from psychiatry at LRMC, that resulted in punishment by my chain of command. I have talked to many soldiers, who have not sought help for their PTSD symptoms, for this very reason. They do not want to damage their military careers.

For the last eighteen months of my military career, I was again stationed at Fort Gordon. My housing was off post because of a housing shortage on post. At my long-term hotel off post, a construction team was also housed. The first thing they did after work was open a case of beer. I was always invited to share. My best support system was my husband Mark, but he was living at our home in Florida. I got to see him about every three to four months. I had no real friends, which is often the case for Reserve soldiers who are pulled out of their home unit and sent to war. I sought help with the mental health team at Fort Gordon because of nightmares, guilt, and excessive drinking. I don't believe that the rest of the anesthesia team had any idea of the mental distress I was experiencing. This time, when I sought help, I was not punished by command. Later in this book, I will discuss the treatment I received at a VAMC in Florida, for my PTSD.

The first poem I ever wrote about my PTSD follows. It was a relief to put the reality down on paper. I would go on to write many more poems about my life with PTSD. I don't think this poem is one of my better writings, but it will begin your acquaintance with the journey a soldier with PTSD takes.

Poem - Post-Traumatic Stress Disorder

She sleeps
In a world of nightmares
Where the wounded keep coming in.

She works
Twenty-six hours straight
In a war that never ends.

She toils
In an operating room
Where the horrors never cease.

She thinks
It would be so easy
Just to let them go.

She wakes
To a pillow soaked in tears
For the ones she couldn't save.

She knows
That the war is forever
Planted in her brain.

She prays
That the night will come
When the dreams will go away.

The Good Times to Remember

MY SISTER BARBARA is the only person who has read all my poems. She was also a Beta Reader for this book. She never made any judgements about my work. However, one day she said to me, "Bev, all of your poems are so sad. Were there never any happy times in the war?" I thought and thought and finally said, "No." But then later, I made myself remember some of the good times.

LRMC was not a military post. It was a large Army medical center perched on a hill in a rather rural area of Germany. Since LRMC had such a small number of military personnel, it was not large enough to have two separate Officers' and Enlisteds' Clubs. We had a Combined Club where all soldiers of any rank and their guests were invited. Karaoke Night at the Combined Club was an especially fun night.

In the winter in Afghanistan, the Taliban refused to fight. They would hunker down in the caves in the mountains near Pakistan. One of the main reasons for not doing winter fighting was that they did not have winter clothing or boots. In Iraq, there would be a "push" to capture a certain city, such as Mosul, Tikrit or Ramadi. After the push and recapture of the city from Al Qaeda control, the American soldiers and coalition fighters would dig in, regroup, resupply and wait for orders to take another city. During the winter in Afghanistan and after a push in Iraq, the number of casualties coming into LRMC would decrease. The usual three planes a day with up to sixty soldiers per plane would drop off. This opened up opportunities for a few days off and time to travel. My husband Mark and I were able to travel around Europe, the Middle East with strict limitations and Africa.

In Southern Germany, in the fall, there were wine walks. Southern Germany is the wine-producing region and vineyards grow along every road. During a wine walk, the roads are closed to traffic except walkers and those riding bicycles, skateboards or rollerblades. Along the roads are booths offering samples from local wineries and booths selling all manner of delicious German food. I was the primary organizer of wine walk trips at LRMC.

The following poem is written for my sister Barbara to make her smile.

The author and a French soldier in Paris

The author and husband Mark in Tunisia

Poem - The Good Times to Remember

I know it causes her such pain
To know what I went through.

She knows it means a lot to me
To have someone to share,
My suffering seems to grow less,
To know that she is there.

One day she smiled and said to me,
"Your poems are so sad.
Please tell me of some happy times
That happened in the war."

I thought and thought and realized
There were some joyful times.
And so this poem is to share
The fun and laughs we had.

I can't forget the crazy times

When we sang at the Club,
My girlfriends were the Supremes group
And I, Diana Ross.

On karaoke night we sang
And we were way off key,
The crowd would laugh and cheer for us
And we thought we were "cool".

When war was slow and injuries down,
I got a few days off.
My husband Mark would make a plan
To go to see the world.

We traveled all over Europe
And to the Middle East,
We even went to Africa
To see the pyramids.

In the fall in South Germany
We went on the wine walks,
We'd gather lots of friends to go
And all jump on the train.

We'd walk the roads of country sides
And sample every wine,
We'd gobble up the German food
For sale along the way.

By end of day we were tipsy
And most of us sunburned.
We'd take the train, sing drinking songs,
While we made the trip home.

My dreams at night take me to war,

The horrors that I saw,
Maybe the dream that comes tonight
Will be a happy one.

The Soldier's Wife

WHEN THE FAMILY of an injured American soldier was quickly flown to Germany after the soldier's arrival at LRMC, this was not a positive omen. It meant that the soldier was not expected to live or had no brain activity. The family was flown over to allow them to have some time with their soldier before his/her death. In the event of no brain activity, the family was asked to turn off life support measures. They were also tactfully encouraged to give permission for organ donation. It was not possible for organs to be usable after a long transport back to the United States, so the organs were given to the Germans. This was much appreciated by the German medical community. Germany has one of the lowest rates of organ donation in Europe. From 2013 to 2017, the number of organ donations carried out in Germany dropped from 1046 to 797. Two thousand people died while waiting for organ donation. In 2019, the German government even drafted a law that would make organ donation compulsory, unless a person opted out. This law is fighting a stiff uphill battle for passage, even though most European countries have a similar law in effect. At LRMC, when we had permission for organ donation, a transplant team from Hamburg, Germany, would arrive to monitor the process and transport the organs. 2005 was the first year the US military allowed organs to be donated by American troops, who had died in Germany from wounds suffered in Iraq and Afghanistan. From 2005-2010, 34 American military members, who died at LRMC, gave 142 organs. In 2010, 10 of the 12 who died at LRMC were donors, giving 45 organs.

A child conceived after the death of an American soldier is called a posthumous child. Some of these children were conceived using sperm that the soldier banked before his deployment. Contemporary medical procedures using Assisted Reproductive Technology (ART) have made it possible for soldiers to conceive genetically related children after death or serious injury. This is done by retrieving and cryopreserving gametes (sperm) or embryos to be used for in vitro fertilization. The exact number of these posthumous children is unknown. Their conception and birth often remain a private and personal matter. The process that has resulted in posthumous children has also resulted in many legal dilemmas, such as inheritance rights and awarding of Social Security benefits. These legal issues are still being decided in the courts.

The following poem tells the story of a young wife, the courageous decision she made, and the posthumous child she bore.

Department of Defense Photo by Staff Sgt. Mary Junell,
NC National Guard

Poem - The Soldier's Wife

I see her in the dim hallway
When I leave the O.R.
A young woman with long dark hair
She stands with distant stare
Out of the window at the trees,
But her sight isn't there.
I think that she sees happy times,
Perhaps her wedding day.

Her husband is in ICU
And I know she's been told,
"There is no hope, it's time to stop
And you must let him go."
Day after day, she stands and stares
Her hair upon her head,
Repeatedly she takes it down,
As if to calm her nerves.

One day she says, "I'll let him go,
But I must have his child."

And so it is arranged for her
And then she lets him die.
We take her soldier to O.R.
For organs she will give,
The part of him that she will have,
The child that she will bear.

I walk out to the long hallway,
The young wife now is gone,
She'll take him home to Arlington,
Full honors burial.
One day she'll take the child of theirs
To see her Daddy's grave.
She'll tell her, "He was brave and true,
A hero in the war."

Another Day at LRMC

DURING MY YEARS of service at LRMC, turnover in staff in the anesthesia department was a constant. Personnel came and went so often that you would miss someone, only to find out they had been gone two weeks or more. Nurse anesthetists from the Army Reserve were being constantly assigned to active duty or released from active duty at LRMC. Their tours of duty could be two weeks, three months, six months or as long as one year. Other nurse anesthetists in the department were being sent to Iraq, to the birthing center we staffed in Italy, on special assignments or on training missions. One such special assignment was to Afghanistan. A team of only females was sent there to provide maternity care for the wife of Hamid Karzai, the President of Afghanistan, on the birth of her first child. This "secret mission" was jokingly called "Operation Royal Vagina" at LRMC. There were also nurse anesthetists who came from the Navy Reserve to serve a one year assignment. Members of the active duty component of the Air Force were also serving in the anesthesia department. Before deployment, many nurse anesthetists from the Reserve component worked in a civilian setting that was devoid of serious trauma. This was a major part of our daily case load. There was often an adjustment period required by new staff in order to cope with the stress of war-time anesthesia care.

The following poem describes one young nurse anesthetist's difficulty in adjusting to the new environment of the trauma center.

U.S. Air Force Photo by Senior Airman Chris Willis

Poem - Another Day at LRMC

My pager beeps, I cannot get ahead,
O.R. is full and more are coming in,
I hurry down the stairwell running fast,
An epidural for a Mom two floors below.

She stands and looks at tarmac by ER,
As wounded soldiers come from who knows where,
She is a newbie where a week is old,
She turns to me her face awash with tears.

I feel a pang of guilt at her distress,
In shock I ask, "Sick?" "Hungry?" or "Just tired?"
To nods of no, she finally replies,
"They just keep coming in. They are so brave."

As Colonel and as boss I've heard it all,
I know that in my heart, I should be kind,
With some compassion I say, "We're at war."
With less compassion I say, "Do your job."

The Puerto Rican Captain

IN THE ARMY RESERVE AND NATIONAL GUARD, the repetitive call-ups to active duty service for the wars in Iraq and Afghanistan have become a way of life. From 2003 to 2006, I received four notifications that I would be called up to active military duty from my civilian job at the VAMC in Bay Pines, Florida. The first call-up was to Fort Gordon, Georgia; the second to Fort Polk, Louisiana (which was subsequently cancelled); the third to Fort Campbell, Kentucky; and the fourth to Heidelberg, Germany (which was subsequently cancelled). This is very disruptive for a soldier and his civilian employer, but is a fact of life accepted by Reserve and National Guard soldiers as part of their military commitment. After three years of call-ups to active duty, I decided to finish my military career with four years of voluntary active duty service.

When I cared for the Puerto Rican National Guard Captain in the next poem, he was on his fifth mobilization to active duty. With that many deployments to a combat zone, chances of survival decrease. It follows the old adage, "Sooner or later your luck runs out". I was grateful that this soldier was finally going home to stay.

Poem - The Puerto Rican Captain

I think about him now and then,
The young Captain was from the Guard,
I asked him first where he was from,
And he said "Puerto Rico, Ma'am.
I'm on my fifth deployment, Ma'am,
I left my six kids with their Mom."
I know he won't go back to war,
He asked "Ma'am, when will I go home?"
I said, "You'll be on the next plane."
I pushed him back to the OR
And then I put him off to sleep,
And when we take his dressing off
The rotten smell, it makes me gag.
I am so angry that I say,
"Who did this work ? The housekeeper?"
Then I feel bad because I know
The MASH team did the best they could.
The surgeon works to clean his stump
And then he neatly wraps it up,
The soldier's arm left in Iraq.

We sent him back to Mom and kids.
I picture him as he plays catch
With smiling kids yelling, "Me, Dad!"
He'll never have to fight again,
At least he went home with his life.

Department of Defense Photo by Petty Officer 1st Class
Kevin Flinn

A Single Combat Boot

AFTER MY TOURS of duty at LRMC and DDEAMC were complete, my four years of active duty were over. I came home from the war and retired at the rank of Colonel with twenty-three years of military service. I was sixty-one years old and weary of war. I returned to my husband in Florida, thinking now I would be fine. I had left the war behind and, mistakenly, thought I would leave PTSD behind. Instead, I had recurring nightmares with yelling and fighting, guilt, depression, irritability, excessive drinking and thoughts of suicide. My marriage was on shaky ground. I finally made the decision to seek help. I went to the VAMC where I had worked as a civilian. It took me three months of constant trying to get help. I was finally assigned to a therapist. She was a fellow in training in psychiatry. She literally saved my life and my marriage. Every week for five months, I had a session utilizing desensitization therapy. This therapy is a treatment that diminishes emotional response to a negative stimulus after repeated exposure to it. This type of therapy was developed in the 1950s and had been used to deal with phobias and anxiety disorders. It has found a place as a treatment for combat PTSD. In the process, I first identified the most upsetting occurrence that I had had in the war. Then I learned relaxation techniques. Next, I wrote and rewrote and talked about the incident in greater detail every week for months. I used my learned relaxation techniques to respond to the incident, until I could recall the event without having all of the negative responses, such as fast heart rate, sweating, panic feelings, inability to catch my breath, crying and shaking. This is a long, painful process that requires a strong commitment. Nobody ever said that dealing with PTSD would be easy. However, it was a very effective therapy for me. I was also prescribed two medications to help me cope, an antidepressant and a sleeping medication. There are many other therapies for the treatment of PTSD, which I will discuss later in this book.

Even after I finished therapy at the VAMC, I continued to have isolated memories from the war that I could not "put to rest". This usually involved particular soldiers with devastating injuries for whom I had provided anesthesia care. Sometimes it was a soldier who did not survive in spite of all my efforts. Memories of these soldiers would run through my mind repetitively. I finally put these thoughts on paper. These random thoughts gradually evolved into this poem collection.

I wrote poetry for two years. Then in 2018, the VAMC sent a mass email to veterans with a request for them to submit their work in a Creative Arts Competition. When I got the email, I thought I had no creative arts, until I saw the poetry category. My poems won first, second and third place at my local VAMC and then a gold medal at the national level. I will discuss later my trip to the National Veterans Creative Arts Festival in Des Moines, Iowa in November 2018.

The poem that follows won first place at Bay Pines VAMC and the gold medal nationally. As long as trauma was coming into the operating room during the war, I kept my emotions in check and did my job. This poem tells of a time of emotional outpouring.

Poem - A Single Combat Boot

Sixteen hours of trauma coming in,
I walk the long dark hallway
Finally going home.

I see a shadow in the distance,
A single combat boot left
Lying on the floor.

I pick it up and clutch it to my chest,
Then collapse in shadowed corner
I break down in tears.

I sob for every soldier
Who needs one.
I sob for every soldier
Who needs none.
I sob for every soldier
Left behind.
I sob for those who never
Will come home.

I sob for mothers who have
Lost a child.
I sob for wife and child who
Grieve alone.
I sob for all of us who
Went to war.
I sob for me who couldn't
Save them all.

I place the boot back gently on the floor,
That soldier doesn't need it anymore,
I walk the long dark hallway,
I am finally going home.

Department of Defense Photo by POWMIA

The Life-Changing Toll of War

ANGER IS OFTEN another component of PTSD. Soldiers with PTSD may feel anger towards: a leader whose judgement they questioned; family or friends, who were less than supportive during their deployment; or themselves, because of the changes in their bodies resulting from injuries or the death of buddies. I experienced anger at the machine of war that resulted in the devastating injuries and deaths that I saw. Some of the injuries I saw in the operating room resulted in the soldier's life never being the same. I was angry at myself because there were soldiers whom I couldn't save. I was angry at the VAMC that had violated my employment rights three times. Not always is the anger of PTSD reasonable, but it is real nonetheless.

The next poem you will read is about a young soldier who came in with critical and devastating injuries. His anesthesia case was particularly difficult. I felt overwhelming anger at the extent of his injuries and the futility of war. I am still working through my acceptance of his fate.

Poem - The Life-Changing Toll
of War

When I went to the I.C.U.
To see the soldier, my next case,
The soldier looked to be asleep,
But he'd been put in a coma.
The coma drugs would let him rest,
And allow time for him to heal.
He was a very handsome man,
There was not one mark on his face,
But from waist down, no part remained,
An IED blast takes its toll.
I heard his father was a doc,
Who was en route to see his son,
I knew that he would be distraught,
To know he'd only half a child.
We brought the soldier to O.R.
To check his wounds and clean them up.
Plastic bags held his body wastes,
All of his man parts blown away,
Of legs, only hip bones remained.
A second trauma surgeon came

And agreed his hip bones must go.
He said, "A source of infection,
No purpose would they ever serve."
And so the surgeons start to work,
Rivers of blood ran down the floor,
And I had to call out, "We must stop,
'Til I can give some to replace."
And after I gave bags of blood,
The process started up again.
I thought back to a time I'd served
In mountains in El Salvador,
In pitch dark, a volcano glowed,
It spewed hot lava down its sides,
Their rivers red like blood would flow.
I was so angry that the war,
Had only sent me half of him.
I often wondered if he lived
On his return to the US.
I wonder if he made a life,
One he could live with after war.

U.S. Army Photo by Sgt. Sara Wood

The Taliban Sniper in Afghanistan

EVEN THOUGH THE Taliban in Afghanistan shied away from fighting in winter, they still managed to wreak havoc on American and coalition soldiers. From their mountain hideaways, they would creep out to snipe at American soldiers on patrol. After years of fighting Russian soldiers and then the American and coalition soldiers, their marksmanship skills were expert.

There was one particular sniper who was a lethal thorn in the side of the American forces. Most of the soldiers he struck did not survive to leave the mountain passes. If the snow storms were deadly, helicopters could not fly into the area to evacuate casualties. The trip down to Bagram Air Base in Kandahar by roads, devastated by years of fighting, could take days. The result was a delay in definitive treatment and infection. I provided care to three of the sniper's casualties, two American soldiers and one British soldier. The young soldier with a devastating infection in the following poem was the incident I used for my desensitization therapy.

The next poem expresses the helplessness, anger and depression I felt, when I cared for those three young men.

Poem - The Taliban Sniper in Afghanistan

I hate the sniper in the hills,
Whose aim is swift and accurate.
When our troops go out on patrol,
He takes them down with one clean shot
And then he hides inside the caves
And waits for his next chance to kill.
He aims below the helmet's rim
To paralyze from the neck down.
I only know of two victims
Who made it out to Landstuhl's doors.
I can't forget the both of them,
One from England, one from U.S.
The British lad was terrified,
Dependent on machine to breath.
He couldn't swallow his own spit
And looked at me with pleading eyes.
The U.S. lad was comatose,
Infected neck from the long trip.
When we brought him to the O.R.,
The plan to stabilize his neck.

The surgeon cautioned me, "Take care,
Lest his head come off in your hands."
We gently turned him on his face,
But there was nothing we could do,
Infection had destroyed all hope.
The sniper changed the game he played,
He'd shoot the soldiers in the face.
I did the case for one soldier,
At the request of surgery team.
Their work took nine tedious hours,
To try to make a face for him.
The next day saw a case the same,
A second one, same injury.
Again the request came to me,
But with regret I just said, "No."
I couldn't face nine hours of grief,
Of knowing that we can't undo,
To know this boy would be deformed,
He'd live a life that is so changed.
The sniper waited in his cave,
One day the Army pinned him down,
The Air Force bombers came that day,
And leveled flat the place he hid.
And I thanked God the man was dead,
But knew that he would be replaced.
I often think of those soldiers,
So many who died from their wounds,
I often think of those who lived,
Did any have a happy life?

Department of Defense Photo by Army Sgt. Liane Hatch

A Veteran's Thoughts

WHEN I CAME HOME from the Iraq/Afghanistan Wars, people thanking me for my service just rubbed me the wrong way. I remember thinking that it was so easy to say, "Thank you for your service," but did they ever reach out to a deployed soldier's family? Did they ever offer to mow their yard, take over a hot meal or offer to babysit for a few hours so a stressed mom or dad could get out? This would have been especially helpful for Reserve soldiers' families, because they do not live on military bases but out in the community. They do not have the support system offered to Active Duty soldiers by a military community.

When I came home from my two short (3-6 months) deployments, I had followed all the rules outlined in the federal USERRA law of 1994. This law protects the employment rights of Reserve soldiers called up to active duty for a deployment. And yes, the law not only states what employers must do, but also the responsibilities of the soldier. Some of the duties of the soldier include giving appropriate notice to the employer of impending call-ups and giving notice quickly in the event the deployment is extended or cancelled. The employer has certain restrictions, such as not forcing the soldier to use vacation time to cover military duty and to reinstate a soldier on his return in a job he/she would have attained if not on military duty. On my three returns to Bay Pines VAMC, my civilian employer, my employment rights were violated. It was necessary for me to call the ESGR and get their assistance in "helping" my employer to understand the law. I was correct in my positions and won the grievances. However, this did not make positive relations between my bosses and me. I served with so many VAMC-employed Reserve soldiers from all over the US who had faced similar problems. These grievances were my prime motivators to volunteer for four years of active duty service to finish my military career. On my last return to my VAMC, I turned in my resignation. I have talked to many soldiers whose civilian employers have violated their USERRA rights. So much for, "Thank you for your service."

After many years, I have become more tolerant. I no longer feel like shouting an obscenity when I see that "Support a Veteran" yellow ribbon on the back of a car. On Memorial Day this year, I put on my uniform to attend the veterans ceremony at the local VAMC. When my husband and I were leaving, a young woman said to me, "Thank you for your service." I smiled at her and said, "You're welcome."

The following poem expresses my feelings on this subject.

Poem - A Veteran's Thoughts

Don't thank me for my service
And then quickly walk away.
Don't glance at my PTSD tattoo
And then avert your eyes.
Don't thank me for your freedom
And then refuse to stand.
I went to war for country
Not for medals, not for rank.
I served beside my brothers
And I don't need your thanks.
I do need you to understand
That I am different now.
War has a way of changing us,
I'll never be the same.
And now we take our own lives
Twenty-one a day.
We go to the VA for help
But there we're turned away.
Most days we feel forgotten

Like no one sees our scars.
It seems like only Veterans' Day
You recognize we're here.

The author on Memorial Day 2019

The Guilt of Promotion

I WAS COMMISSIONED as an officer in the Army Nurse Corps in 1988. I went in at the rank of First Lieutenant. I took all the Army courses that were required for promotion. It was also necessary to maintain all my soldier readiness skills, such as passing physical fitness tests and maintaining weapons qualifications. I was assigned to positions of increasing authority with more soldiers to command. An Officer Effectiveness Report is an evaluation of the soldier done yearly. It is the primary document looked at by the promotion board to determine a soldier's eligibility for promotion. I was promoted to Captain, then Major and then Lieutenant Colonel. While I was serving at LRMC, I was preparing for and sending my promotion packet to the Colonel board. This is an extremely selective board. An officer wants absolutely nothing to make a negative impact. This includes reporting a sexual assault. In the military, being a victim of sexual assault is an embarrassment.

As a Lieutenant Colonel and Colonel, I began to feel that doing all the right things were not enough to earn a promotion. I started to think that the load of guilt an officer could carry weighed heavily in the board's decision. When I was in charge of the operating room, I decided which emergency case would take priority. One day, a neurosurgeon came charging into the OR demanding an operating room immediately. Every room I had was in use. He yelled at me that if the soldier needing the OR died, it would be all my fault. That was the day I decided promotion was based on the amount of guilt you could bear. That was also the day I decided to retire after the completion of my active duty tour.

The next poem will give you insight into the promotion process.

Poem - The Guilt of Promotion

From 1st Loo-ey to Captain,
From Captain then to Major,
I dotted all my I's
And I crossed all my T's.

The thought that rank was merit based
Was what I had believed.
Promotion was achieved by those,
Who earned it as their due.

And then the war came,
My life changed,
As did my view of rank.

I trained my soldiers in their skills,
Then sent them off to war,
And then I followed them to war,
And lived the hell they lived.

From Major then to LTC,

From LTC to Colonel,
The way to rank was based on guilt,
How much you could absorb.

I sent my soldiers off to war,
They died and I felt blame,
I couldn't save them, watched them die,
The guilt became a stone.

I put on my beret one day,
The mirror where I checked,
My face was looking back at me,
My eyes were filled with guilt.

That was the day I made the choice,
To take my guilt and go,
I turned in my retirement form,
And then I walked away.

U.S. Army Photo by Elizabeth Fraser

Christmas at LRMC

FOR THE TWO and a half years I was stationed at LRMC, I volunteered to provide the emergency anesthesia coverage for both Christmases. Mark and I had no family in Germany. Most of the staff in the anesthesia department were stationed in Germany with their families and many had small children. My voluntary duty gave them an opportunity to spend the holidays with their little ones. At Christmastime, most of the Taliban were holed up in caves in the mountains awaiting the spring thaw. As a result, we didn't receive our usual daily increment of casualties from Afghanistan. However, it seemed that al Qaeda in Iraq knew that Christmas was a very special holiday for the American and coalition soldiers. They tried hard to up the number of casualties coming into LRMC. The soldiers stationed downrange had a difficult time during the Christmas holiday dealing with separation from families and friends. Sometimes their depression led to suicide attempts.

The next poem is about a young soldier and his parents, whom I encountered in the ICU on Christmas Day. My heart broke for the parents of this young man. They were receiving the devastating news that no parent ever wants to hear.

Poem - Christmas at LRMC

I volunteered for the two years
To cover Christmas in O.R.
In Germany, just Mark and me,
No family to share the joy.
It gave those soldiers who had kids,
Some days off to have Christmas cheer.
On Christmas Day O.R. was slow,
Just one case on for afternoon.
Things had been quiet for a while,
But planes were coming from Iraq.
Taliban in Afghanistan
Were in the hills near Pakistan.
They didn't fight in winter cold,
But waited for the spring to thaw
The windswept mountains in their land.
Al Queda didn't share that view,
They saw Christmas as their big day
To kill as many of our troops,
A Christmas gift to the U.S.

And so I went to ICU
To see the soldier we would do,
As I stood outside of his room,
I saw a group at the next door.
I read my soldier's history,
While listening to the group near me.
The trauma surgeon kindly said,
To Mom and Dad, "He is brain dead.
We ask you now to please donate
Organs for which he has no use,
And then you must just let him go."
I saw his mother gasp in shock
And slowly sink down to the floor.
A chair was quickly brought to her,
A place where she could sit and cry.
My thoughts went back to a sad day
When I was told my son was dead.
I felt the mother's pain and grief
As if it were just yesterday.
Their son had come in from Iraq,
He'd put a gun against his head,
Depressed that war would just not end.
The tears were streaming down my face,
I couldn't read the page of print.
I thought I've got to leave this place,
Back to O.R. to hide my grief.
My sergeant saw me and was shocked,
And with concern he questioned me,
"Are you OK? What can I do?"
I couldn't even answer him,
And so he took me in his arms.
He said, "I'm sorry you're so sad."
We just don't do what he just did,
In military, we don't touch.
It was so kind of him to try

To offer comfort in that way.
And later when I left O.R.,
In ICU the group was gone.
I finished what I'd come to do,
The surgeon went to do his work,
The parents gone to grieve alone.

The LRMC Emergency Team Christmas Day 2007

The Last Photo

ALL THE POEMS I have written were about my wartime experiences, until the poem I wrote about my son Kevin. I attended the National VA Creative Arts Festival in Des Moines, Iowa in November 2018. I will devote a chapter later in this book to that experience. While at the workshop, we fifteen gold medal writers spent most of our days in writing workshops. The workshops were meant to help us improve our writing skills. The workshop coordinator was a man from Walter Reed Army Medical Center in Washington, DC. There he offered writing therapy for PTSD.

At the Festival, I became friends with a Vietnam veteran who had recently started therapy for PTSD. He used writing to deal with his symptoms and was a gold medal winner. This veteran also had a serious debilitating disease. His wife usually accompanied him to assist with his mobility. One morning, his lovely wife was not with him. He sat opposite me in the workshops. As we received our next writing assignment, I could see his anxiety increasing. At a break, I talked to my friend privately. I told him I was feeling anxious about the assignment. I told him that if either one of us needed to leave the room during our writing, the other would follow. Then, together, we would diffuse the anxiety. He smiled in relief at my proposal.

The assignment was to write about a photo you cherished. I had never written anything about my youngest child, but my last photograph of Kevin is a cherished possession. As I wrote my poem "The Last Photo", the tears rolled down my face and I was stifling sobs. I quietly got up from my chair and left the room, sat down on a chair in the hallway and sobbed. Then I felt a comforting arm around my shoulders. My friend had also left the room, just as we had planned. Only it was he who had come to my rescue, instead of vice versa. This is an example of what veterans do for each other. The following quote by Vera Nazarian tells of veterans helping veterans and soldiers lifting up other soldiers:

"Was it you or I who stumbled first? It does not matter. The one of us who finds the strength to get up first, must help the other."

Thank you so much, Ray, for being there for me.

Poem - The Last Photo

The photo of my son Kevin
Was taken on Thanksgiving Day,
He's standing in a silly pose,
In ragged jeans and old sweatshirt,
He's laughing at the camera,
My youngest child was such a ham,
And three months later he was dead,
Snatched at fourteen in a car wreck,
He was one of three killed that day,
He joined his sister in God's hands.
And at his wake the people came,
Told me they loved him; held my hand,
We buried him beside my Dad,
I can't remember much of that.
The photo sits on the bureau,
Each week I clean and pick it up,
I look into his smiling face,
I always say, "I love you, kid."
He always was a "party guy",
The life of every social group,

I know that he's in heaven now,
He's party planner for the Lord.
I put the photo on the shelf,
I dust and sweep and think of him,
And I go on.

The last photo taken of the author's son, Kevin, aged 14

My Friend Laura, Nurse Anesthetist

MY BEST FRIEND at LRMC was a nurse anesthetist named Laura. We were pretty much inseparable. Since Reserve soldiers were always treated like second class citizens by the active duty soldiers, Laura and I were always working hard to prove our worth. We also fought for Reserve soldiers rights in the active duty arena. If, for some reason, I needed to switch my day off or trade off emergency call days, Laura was my go to person for the request. I did the same for her. For two and a half long years, we served together. We always had each other's back. When the casualties coming in were overwhelming and the stress was at its highest, we would come together at night in our housing. We would share a glass of wine, discuss very difficult cases and talk about life after war. After I left LRMC, I did a final year of active duty in Georgia and Laura went to Iraq, which was an assignment she had requested. I haven't heard from Laura since.

The next poem is about and dedicated to my amazing friend.

Poem - My Friend Laura, Nurse Anesthetist

It seemed that we were Mutt and Jeff,
I was so tall while she was short,
I was so thin while she was stout,
But that is where the difference ends.
We shared the same rank in the Corps,
We both came from Army Reserve,
We volunteered to go to war,
We served at LRMC for two years,
Her name was Laura, my best friend.
We fought for rights for the Reserve,
When we were treated second-class
By Active soldiers we outranked,
We worked to prove we're just as good.
After long days with little sleep,
When planes came in three times a day
Bringing the wounded from the wars,
I'd sit at night in darkened room
And sip my wine and think of home,
Then there's a soft knock on my door,
There Laura stands with glass in hand.

We'd sit and talk of soldiers lost,
The guilt for those we couldn't save.
We'd talk of family we had left,
Her teen-age girls back in the States.
We'd pray for soldiers everywhere,
We'd pray for us and war to end.
After two years our time was up,
I went Stateside for one more year,
My friend Laura went to Iraq.
I think of her from time to time,
How we retired, went on with life.
She always seemed more tough than me,
Do we both have PTSD?
I never heard from her again,
I guess war was our only bond.

U.S. Navy Photo by Chief Petty Officer Josh Ives

Nighttime and PTSD

I HAVE WRITTEN a number of poems about my life with PTSD. I've written about my symptoms and the treatment I have received. It seems that nighttime is the most difficult time to cope with the past. When it is dark and quiet, the memories seem to flood my mind. Experiences that I thought were buried, come back in flashes. The nighttime is also when the nightmares of war destroy my sleep and wake me up in terror. Since I have received extensive treatment for my PTSD, the nights have markedly improved. Now, it is very seldom that I go "back to the war" in my dreams. If you are suffering any of the symptoms outlined in the last chapter of this book, whether it be from combat, sexual assault or other trauma, I beg you to get help. There is so much help available. I also hope that, eventually, you have peaceful sleep.

Poem - Nighttime and PTSD

At night I go back to the war,
My eyes are shut but still I see
The flashing pictures of my life,
The faces of the ones I lost.
I take a pill to block this out,
But memories are just too strong.
I hear the moans of soldiers' pain,
I smell the reek of burning flesh,
I dread the copters coming in,
I feel the nausea in my gut,
And then I pray "Please, take me home".
When I wake up and face the truth,
My heart is pounding in my chest,
I cannot breath, where is the air?
The tears of anguish soak my face.
I used to think that time would heal,
But now I know the war goes on.
I try to stay awake for fear
My dreams will take me back again.

I know that there are many more
Who face the terror just like me.
I wish them hope, I wish them joy,
I wish them nights of peaceful sleep.

U.S. Marine Corps Photo by Cpl. Carlos Lopez

My Aussie Girl Soldier

MULTI-NATIONAL FORCE-IRAQ (MNF-I), often referred to as the coalition forces, was a military command during the 2003 invasion of Iraq and much of the ensuing Iraq War. These soldiers fought alongside the American soldiers in Iraq. The MNF-I replaced the previous force, Combined Joint Task Force 7, in May 2004. It was later reorganized into its successor, United States Forces - Iraq in January 2011. There were 21 countries represented in the coalition forces. 317 coalition soldiers lost their lives in Iraq while the American forces had 4,486 deaths. As of May 2011, all coalition soldiers had withdrawn from Iraq. On December 18, 2011, the U.S. forces withdrew, thus bringing an end to the Iraq War.

Following the terrorist attacks of September 11, 2001, several nations took on the Taliban and Al-Qaeda in Afghanistan during Operation Enduring Freedom (OEF). OEF was the initial combat operations starting on October 7, 2001. There were many countries who sent forces and provided other forms of support to the American forces. Some nations' operations continued as part of NATO's International Security Assistance Force. As of July 27, 2018, there have been 2,372 U.S. military deaths in Afghanistan. As of August 5, 2018, there have been 1,145 coalition deaths there. After thirteen years, on December 28, 2014, President Barack Obama announced the end of OEF. Continued operations in Afghanistan by the US military forces, both non-combat and combat, now occur under the name Operation Freedom's Sentinel. The War in Afghanistan continues to this day. For every one death in the Iraq and Afghanistan Wars, there were approximately eight injuries. These ranged from minor to devastating, life-changing injuries.

We rarely saw an Australian casualty from Iraq. My husband Mark and I traveled to Australia some years after I returned from my wartime service. We visited a beautiful Soldier's Memorial in Sydney. I told the curator we had taken care of the Australian soldiers in the Iraq War. Mark and I were immediately treated like celebrities. We were given heartfelt thanks and gifts.

The following poem is about a young Australian soldier and her joy at going home.

Poem - My Aussie Girl Soldier

Her head was covered tightly
In a bloody dressing roll,
Her tiny face was childlike,
Out of place in this big war.

She seemed too young to be here,
I remember that I said,
"What's a pretty little girl
Doing in an ugly war?"

She said, "Ma'am, I'm a soldier,
And I came to fight this war!"
She said "I am an Aussie,
And I dream of going home."

We took her to the O.R.
And her forehead was a hole,
I was shocked by the damage,
Since she'd been so wide awake.

The surgeon worked his magic,
As he tried to make her whole,
I said, "She's a fragile thing
And war will take its toll."

In Clothes Closet I asked for things,
My husband looked askance,
For frilly PJs and lipstick
Were very strange requests.

Last time I saw my Aussie girl
In PJs with pink lips,
She laughed and smiled and said to me,
"Thank you for your care
And thank you for the love you showed.
I'll tell them all back home,
I'm finally leaving war behind,
I'm finally coming home."

Living with PTSD and The Long, Long Road

THE LAST TWO poems in this collection deal with my struggles with PTSD and the hope I can offer other veterans. When I started having symptoms of PTSD in 2008, I was an active duty soldier. Admitting to this problem and seeking help was very risky. There was a stigma connected to seeking help, that could negatively impact a soldier's career. I seriously weighed the potential consequences of requesting treatment. I believe the military branches have made some effort to combat the negative ramifications of asking for treatment for PTSD, but there is still much to be done. The VA is also directing an effort to meeting veterans' mental health needs. However, this has not resulted in a decrease in the number of veteran suicides.

Dealing with PTSD is neither an easy nor instant process. It often requires a lengthy commitment and multi-faceted approach. In the last chapter of this book, I will discuss PTSD and treatment options. The number of veteran and service member suicides per year is heartbreaking. 21 veterans and servicemembers a day take their own lives. This is a tragedy that must be stopped.

Poem - Living with PTSD

I never know when they will come,
The memories of the war I saw,
A certain sight, a certain smell
Will make it all come crashing down.
At night I live the war again,
I kick and fight and yell the names
Of all the soldiers I have known.
Sometimes I hear the call for help,
"All transport teams to the E.R."
And then I know the planes are here,
That carry wounded from the war.
Some nights I dream of the O.R.,
I work for hours to save the lives.
I know that I don't save them all,
I grieve for soldiers I have lost.
When I wake up, I'm drenched in sweat,
My heart is pounding in my chest,
My pillowcase is soaked with tears,
But then I know it's just a dream,
I dread to sleep, relive the scenes.

When I sought treatment at VA,
My doctor said, "We'll beat this thing,"
And so for months we worked on me,
Used her techniques to ease the pain,
And now I find that life is good.
I take my meds and write these words,
And I refuse to take my life,
To join the twenty-one per day.
If you are fighting demons too,
Please get some help, don't walk alone.
I go to battle everyday,
I live with Post-Traumatic Stress,
But it won't take my joy away.

Poem - The Long Long Road

I hope one day my memories
Will blur and fade, then go away.

I pray one day the faces of
The ones I lost etched in my brain
Will finally be put to rest.

I wish that nights would just hold sleep,
Not flashes of the war I fought
And I would wake and be at peace.

It has been a long, long road
Of ups and downs and back and forth
And haunting thoughts, survivor's guilt.

First medications for the grief,
Then therapy and poetry
And talks about the toll of war.

I know that there are thousands who

Fight the same battle, just like me,
And twenty-one are lost each day.

They think I just can't live like this
And in despair, they take their life,
A sad statistic left behind.

The memories are vicious things,
They tear and shred and steal your joy
Until you get the help you need.

There is a life that follows war,
When family and friends are there,
They want us to be whole again.

I beg you if you feel alone,
Know there is help awaiting you,
So please reach out and take its hand.

I hope one day your memories
Will blur and fade, then go away.

National Veterans Creative Arts Festival

BY THE SPRING OF 2018, I had been writing poetry for two years. My poems were very personal and only shared with my sister, Barbara. She read them all and accepted the feelings I expressed as a necessary part of my dealing with my wartime experiences. Then I received an e-mail sent out to all veterans from the VA Healthcare System. It was a call for entry submissions to their local VAMC Creative Arts Competition. I initially thought that I had no creative arts to enter, until I read through the available categories. The writing category included poetry. I pondered whether I wanted to share my poetry and display my PTSD and pain to other people. I finally decided to take the chance.

I entered three poems in the poetry writing category at Bay Pines VAMC in Florida. A short while later, I learned that I had won a first, second and third place ribbon for my entries. This was a wonderful affirmation that my poetry had value. My first place winning poem "A Single Combat Boot" was submitted to the national competition. I was thrilled to learn that I had won a gold medal.

Bay Pines VAMC contacted me to ask if I would like to attend the National VA Creative Arts Festival in Des Moines, Iowa. I readily agreed. My trip was completely paid for by Veterans Affairs. So on October 31, my husband Mark and I flew to Des Moines. Thus began one of the most heartwarming experiences of my life.

The Festival was sponsored by the Des Moines VAMC and the American Legion Auxiliary, who treated the veteran participants and their families like VIPs. I had the opportunity to meet and share experiences with veterans from all over the United States. There were non-stop activities to attend, such as daily writing workshops, an evening coffee house where the writers read their work and a trip to the Capitol Annex where the writers talked about and signed their work for hundreds of visitors. The performers and artists were involved in many activities related to their specialty. On the last day of the Festival, the performers staged a three-hour Broadway-worthy show. The highlight of the Festival, however, was meeting, getting to know and sharing experiences with other veterans. There was a warm feeling of comradery, acceptance and love.

I am already making plans for next year's competition. If you are not on the email link to your local VAMC, contact the Recreation Therapy Department there for information about their Creative Arts Competition. I hope to see you at the next National VA Creative Arts Festival. More information can be found at https://www.blogs.va.gov/nvspse/national-veterans-creative-arts-festival.

The author receiving First Place for her poem "A Single Combat Boot" at the 2018 National VA Creative Arts Festival

Veteran PTSD and Suicide

WHEN I ATTENDED the 2018 National VA Creative Arts Festival, I wanted to not only attend but to help other veterans. I had thought about this for a long time and then read an article about the veteran suicide rate. I had been dismayed for months about the current 20.6 veteran and servicemember suicides per day. I knew the statistics but where was the solution to stopping this epidemic? So I have made it my mission to prevent more suicide deaths. I went to the Festival with a three page handout. The first page evolved into the cover for this book. The second and third pages were an informational guide entitled "Fact Sheet for Veteran PTSD and Suicide". I distributed 400 handouts. I told people that, if they knew a veteran or soldier who needed help, to give them the handout. My hope is that this book will serve as a resource for those needing treatment for PTSD and depression.

The VA Healthcare System is striving to offer quicker and more comprehensive treatment. So much more needs to be done. Nineteen suicides occurred on VA campuses from October 2017 to November 2018 - seven of them in parking lots. A 55 year-old Marine Colonel shot himself in December 2018 in the parking lot at Bay Pines VAMC, a facility two blocks from my home in Florida. This loss of life <u>must</u> stop.

A copy of the handout is included. Please feel free to copy and share it with anyone who could benefit. I have also included some resources that may be helpful to veterans and servicemembers needing PTSD treatment or suicide prevention.

If you know veterans or servicemembers, who are dealing with PTSD, reach out to them, be a good listener and assist them in seeking treatment. The epidemic of suicides among veterans and servicemembers requires an effort from all of us.

Fact Sheet for Veteran PTSD and Suicide

Definition of PTSD: Serious mental illness characterized by symptoms of avoidance and nervous system arousal after experiencing or witnessing a traumatic event.

Risk factors for development of PTSD in veterans: Longer times at war, lower level of education, more severe combat conditions, female gender, racial minority status, lower rank, prior psychological problems and lack of social support.

Statistics: 500,000 troops who served in Iraq/Afghanistan over past 13 years have been diagnosed with PTSD. 31% Vietnam, 10% Desert Storm, 11% Afghanistan and 20% Iraq War veterans have PTSD.

Symptoms: Intrusion (ex. nightmares, flashbacks), Avoidance (ex. distressing memories or feelings), Negative cognition and mood (ex. fear, guilt, detachment), and Arousal (ex. aggressiveness, sleeplessness, self-destructive behavior).

There is help available.

Recovery steps: 1) Get moving – Get regular exercise (ex. running, swimming), pursue outdoor activities (ex. hiking, mountain biking, rock climbing).

2) Self-regulate your nervous system – Mindful breathing, yoga,

meditation, sensory input (ex. music therapy, canine therapy, equestrian therapy).

3) Connect with others - Volunteer, join PTSD support group, talk with others who care.

4) Take care of your body – Relaxation techniques, blow off steam (ex. boxing), healthy diet, get plenty of sleep, avoid alcohol, drugs and nicotine.

5) Deal with flashbacks, nightmares and intrusive thoughts – State to yourself the reality, describe what you see, use a simple script, try tapping your arms.

6) Work through survivor's guilt: Honestly assess your responsibility and role, channel guilt into positive activity.

7) Seek professional treatment – Cognitive Behavioral Therapy (CBT), Prolonged Exposure Therapy ((PET), medication, Eye movement Desensitization and Reprocessing (EMDR), acupuncture, medical marijuana.

Suicide Risk: 20.6 veterans, active duty, Guard and Reserve commit suicide/day. Total suicides 7,519/yr.

2005-2016 saw 26% increase in veteran deaths by suicide; 2001-2014 saw 62% increase in women vets.

Suicide rate among young veterans (age 18-35) increased 10% in 2017.

Combat veterans are more likely to have suicidal ideation. Associated with PTSD and depression.

70% use firearms (very effective method).

Veterans Crisis Line: 1-800-273-8255

National Suicide Prevention Lifeline: 1-800-273-8255, Veterans press 1

OR text SIGNS to 741741 for the Crisis Text Line

Resources for PTSD Treatment

WHEN I STARTED treatment for my PTSD in 2008, there were very few treatments available. My choices were medication, talk therapy or a combination of the two. At that time, talk therapy was a sit-down visit with a psychiatrist or psychologist to discuss the possible causes of your PTSD and symptoms for a 60-90 minute period. When I was stationed in Germany at LRMC and at DDEMAC for my last tour of duty, I chose the combination therapy.

PTSD therapy has three main goals:

- Improve your symptoms
- Teach you skills to deal with it
- Restore your self-esteem.

By the time I returned home and retired from the Army in 2011, the modalities of trauma-focused psychotherapies had expanded to: Cognitive Behavioral Therapy, Prolonged Exposure Therapy, Eye Movement Desensitization and Reprocessing and Group Therapy. When I sought help in 2010 at a VAMC, it was a long and arduous process to get treatment. I was on medication and had CBT, which involves a 12 week course of treatment with 60-90 minute sessions and PE, which involves 8 to 15 weeks of 90 minute sessions to achieve these three goals. My sessions were two hours long for 20 weeks. This seems like a big commitment of time and effort. In the larger picture, it was 20 weeks to get my life and marriage back. My therapy saved me from drug and alcohol addiction and death.

I don't believe there is a "total cure" for PTSD, be it the result of war, sexual assault, witnessing a mass shooting, natural disasters or childhood abuse. There are still good and bad days and nights even after treatment. A commitment to long term therapy, such as group therapy, may be required. However, the bad days and nights are much fewer and less intense. Life becomes a joy to live again.

Since my days in therapy, a wealth of new treatments have shown positive results. Many health professionals have begun to include complementary alternative therapies into their treatment regimens. Some methods that have been used include:

- Relaxation techniques such as yoga, mindfulness and meditation, massage and deep breathing
- Aqua therapy
- Acupuncture
- Canine and equine therapy
- Stress Inoculation Therapy (SIT)
- Creative therapy such as writing, art, music and crafts
- Rhythmic exercise
- Medical marijuana
- Hypnosis
- Addiction treatment
- Acceptance and Commitment Therapy (ACT)

This is not an exhaustive list. New and effective treatments are being published frequently. There is no one treatment fits all. It my be necessary to try different or combinations of treatment before a good fit is found for you. The first step is to recognize your symptoms and seek help. This is the way to take back your life.

I have included information about some resources that are available and their contact information. Your area of the country may offer unique therapies, such as rock climbing or nature hikes. The National Resource Directory (nrd.gov) has more than 14,000 vetted resources available to you and your family.

The loss of life associated with untreated PTSD and depression must stop. Veterans, servicemembers, their families and communities must work together. We can no longer tolerate the loss of 20.6 veterans and servicemembers per day.

Excellent resources can also be found at:

www.22Kill.com – connections to general therapies and treatments, including service animals

www.pstd.va.gov – National Center for PTSD

www.ptsd.va.gov/understand_tx/ - the publication "Understanding PTSD"

Donation of Profits

A COPY of this book will be given free to any veteran or service-member who feels that it may be helpful in their journey with PTSD or depression. I hope that by reading this book, you can see the journey of a veteran with the "Invisible Wounds of War". That veteran sought help and now has a very happy life.

In the event that I realize any profit from the sale of this book, all monies will be equally divided and donated to the following two organizations:

1) Give An Hour - Works to match military and veterans struggling with mental health and well-being issues with a volunteer health professional who can help them recover. They have provided 210,000 hours of service with over 858 active volunteers and 390 partner organizations. Care provided is strictly confidential and <u>cost free</u>. This organization has a 4 Star rating by Charity Navigator. Give An Hour can be reached at www.giveanhour.org

2) Hope for the Warriors - Provides comprehensive support programs for service members, veterans and military families that are focused on transition, health and wellness, peer engagement and connections to community resources. 90.1% of every dollar raised goes directly to programs and services for the warrior community. Support from Hope for the Warriors can be applied for at www.hopeforthewarriors.org or at 1-877-246-7349

These organizations have been recognized by Veterans Advantage for the quality of services they deliver to our nation's veterans.

About the Author

COL(Ret.) Beverly Smith-Tillery grew up in a small town in Kentucky. She worked as a registered nurse for twenty years while raising her three sons. Late in her nursing career, she became a nurse anesthetist. She practiced nurse anesthesia for twenty years prior to her retirement in 2015.

COL Smith-Tillery was commissioned in the US Army in 1988 at the age of 38 and served for 23 years, retiring in 2011 at the age of 61. She has joked that she was the oldest soldier serving in the Iraq/Afghanistan Wars. She watched her brother struggle with PTSD for years after his service in the Vietnam War. Her struggles with PTSD led her to treatment from 2008-2013. She moderates her symptoms now with poetry writing. She was a gold medal winner in the National VA Creative Arts Competition in 2018. She currently shares her time between Florida and Kentucky with her husband Mark Tillery. She would love to hear from you at: woundsandredemption@gmail.com.

Made in the USA
Middletown, DE
09 March 2022

62312626R00076